LOVER'S
LEAP

RAGING
RIVER

THE GOLDEN
TABLE

HAPPY
OAKS

Embracing the Tempest

OTHER WORKS
BY THE AUTHOR

To Fight Fire with Sun

EMBRACING THE TEMPEST

D. A. ANDREWS

Cover Illustration by aerroscape.

Edited by Shelby Leigh.

Book Design & Layout by R. Clift.

SQUIRREL HOUSE PUBLISHING

Edited by Shelby Leigh

Book Design & Layout by R. Clift

Squirrel House Publishing

ISBN: 9781951882129

@daandrews_

For Courtney-Claire and Alexander Lyn:
Thank you for teaching me
how to embrace this tempest
we call life –
even while going overboard

PREFACE

Life has a funny way of demanding to be felt. Has a funny way of kicking you while you are down and expecting you to learn from the punches, get up, dust yourself off. I was born and raised in Jamaica and while some of my upbringings are universal, other parts are unique to my own existence. Over the years, I have sent myself to several therapists – an insatiable hunger for any kind of knowledge on how to navigate life settled deep within my core.

I am a woman of habit, and it took me years to learn the lessons that I have portrayed in the following pages. It has taken me years to become okay with being vulnerable and airing my "dirty laundry".

I have always had a fascination with water despite the deep fear that it will be my undoing. I retreat to my shower on days I need to feel alive, dip my toes in the ocean when I feel a need to clear my head. Water has been a consistent source of comfort for me over the years.

In the pages that follow, I share with you what has made me the woman I am today. All the thoughts, fears, and feelings I have encountered along my journey and still struggle with today.

My therapist was the first person to teach me about feelings coming in waves. She was also the first person to teach me how to embrace them instead of fighting them. How to release control in the midst of the tempest of our emotions and allow it to just be observed.

This is the purpose of this book. To show how I have embraced the tempest of my life while becoming myself. I hope you take these thoughts with you as you read through the following pages. I kept the language close to the form of English I learned as I believe it allows me to present myself entirely as I am. Without any form of editing.

I hope you learn of my life as I have experienced it and take from this book the lessons I have learned along the way.

And, more than anything, I hope you learn how to embrace the tempest of emotions in your life. Know that I have extended my hand to keep you company as you read these pages.

Know that you are seen.

With love always,

D. A. Andrews

ACKNOWLEDGMENTS

As this book came to fruition, several people shined their light on me along the way.

To CC, thank you for being there from day one. Thank you for standing by my side and pushing me to keep writing.

To Alex, I will always write these books for you. Thank you for being my source of inspiration.

To Thomas, thank you for always asking me if I have written today. Thank you for supporting me along the way. I love you.

To Savi, here is the second book you have been asking me for! Thank you for always believing in my writing.

To Heidi, thank you for teaching me to embrace the tempest of my emotions and that they come in waves.

To Shelby Leigh, Rachel Clift, Micah, and aerroscape, thank you for being a part of this journey.
I would not be here without you.

LESSON #453

When I was three I held
on to my mother's pants as she walked
out of my classroom, then scooped myself
up and stuck my head in my knapsack,
pretending to search for math homework
as I wiped away my tears.

I repeated these motions
over the years as people left,
retreating to a closet or darkened
room to wipe my tears and nurse
my broken nails and bloodied fingers.

Quite often, I hold on too tightly
to the things or people I love
to the point of suffocation. I don't know
what it means to be okay with uncertainty
nor am I fully okay with the act
of loosening my grip and letting go.

My fear of abandonment
is the most consistent
thing in my life, to the point
where I don't particularly know
how to feel anything else.

Going with the flow does not exist
in my bones. I fear that if I don't cup
my palms around the answers I seek,
they will flutter away into nothingness.
My skin trembles day in, day out
as I am forced to sit back, be patient,
let things unfold as they should.

I.   Life has become one
      tower card moment after another.
      I have learned to pick up
      the pieces only to have them
      fall once again.

II.   I feel like my purpose
      is to teach others how to love,
      but never to receive the same
      in return.

III. Each day I fight tooth and nail
      to understand the lessons
      that present themselves to me.
      Each day the universe leads me
      back to you.

                    — *Just some morning thoughts*

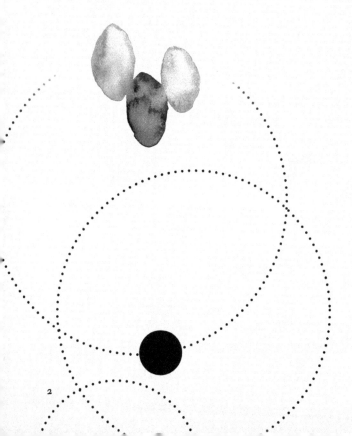

CHRISTMAS DINNER

We gather around the dining table—
the way we do once a year—
dressed to hell in Sunday's best.

My mother emerges from the kitchen with
ham in hand, places it in the center
of the wooden table, smooths the off-white
tablecloth and ignores the curry stain
my sister left there last Christmas.

We hold hands while my father says grace.
My sister and I try to keep our eyes closed,
be reverent, but the roast chicken
and potato salad are in front of us.

My grandmother commends my father
on his rice; he says he learned from the best.
They hand out smiles to each other
as they bite down on their tongues.

My mother passes me a slice of fruit cake:
"Only one. You're getting fat."
I don't make a fuss. Maybe, this time,
she doesn't realize what she said.

She packs the food in containers,
places foil over the ham,
assigns my sister and me to kitchen duty.

My father and grandmother head upstairs
while my mother removes the tablecloth,
puts it in the washing machine with clothes
from the hamper, tries to scrub out the stains
to get it ready for next year.

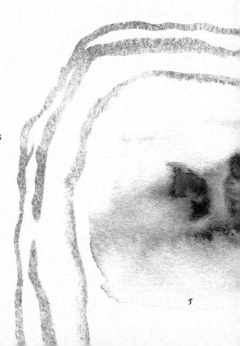

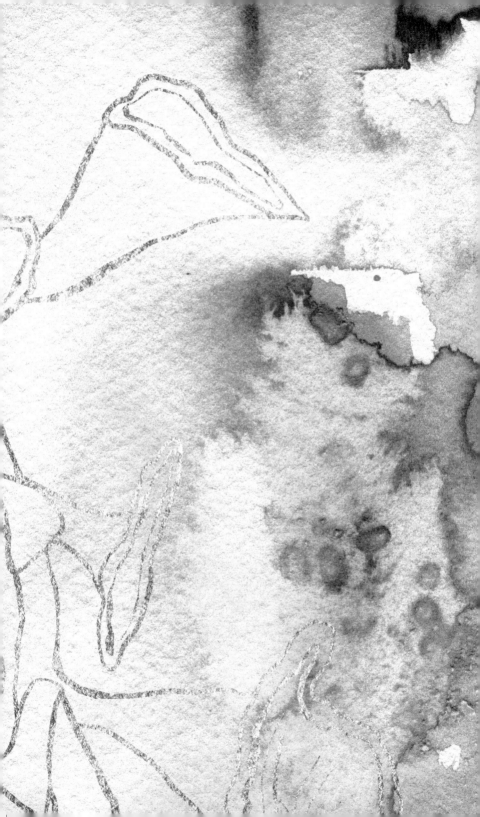

MS. MABLE

She exhales deeply, bends
at the waist, hands on her knees
as she slowly lowers herself
on the stool, fruit and ground provisions
displayed on the blue plastic
laid beneath her feet.

Crowds of people pass by
shuffling through the market;
day in day out she bellows
"Hundred for a pound of yam"
loud enough and often enough
for it to be her anthem.

Her feet press deeply into the pink
meshed bed slippers two sizes
too small, callused heels spilling
over the edge as she beckons
for her Almighty God
to take the case and give her
the pillow.*

She has several mouths to feed,
clothes to put on their backs,
a bad heart and worse lungs.
Yet still, she calls out at the top
of them:
"Hundred for a pound of yam.
Two-fifty for three."

*Jamaican saying: *Tek di case an gimmi di pillow.*
Take the case and give me the pillow.
Meaning akin to "Jesus, take the wheel."

ELAINE

I found my grandmother
in the old find-a-word puzzles
she often focused on. The only way
we got a glimpse into what
went on in her mind.

She circled the words the pages
asked for in red, made drawings
on the inside of the covers in blue,
wrote her name in old cursive
across the title page in black.

Secrets were her currency, often
exchanging love for the latest gossip;
I often did not know if her love
was genuine or a matter of survival.

She passed away last year,
crippled my father and sister
in the process—even my mother,
bless her heart, often shunned by her
during her living years, broke down
several times.

I have yet to find the word
grief in the pages of the find-a-word
book—but if I do,
I will be sure to circle it in red.

B	A	T	T	Z
P	O	I	F	U
Q	U	E	E	N
C	G	A	M	O
O	R	R	A	T
P	I	E	Y	E
V	E	J	B	E
U	D	Z	X	I

Rat	*Grief*	*Bat*	*Rye*	*Ear*
Queen	*Note*	*Tie*	*Pie*	*Cop*

MEGAN LEE

She walks into our 5th grade classroom,
dark blue tunic two sizes too big,
her crushed shirt coloured like the edges
of an old book. Her head hangs, eyes sweep
the ground as she darts to her seat.

Her hair is parted down the middle,
each section in a large plait for
the fifth time this week. She rests
her head on the desk, arms guard
against crumpled pieces of paper
David throws across the classroom;
Ms. James isn't here to shield her.

A man storms into the classroom,
head held high, charcoal hair slicked away
from the heart-shaped face she shares.
His sleeves rolled up to his shoulders,
arms riddled with bulging veins. He barks
her name.

She jumps, pushing the seat away, too slow
to shield her face from his hand; she stumbles
to the ground. This is enough to silence us.

Eleven years, countless Facebook searches,
a class reunion, I can't find her anywhere.

I'm not sure if her father ever took it too far.

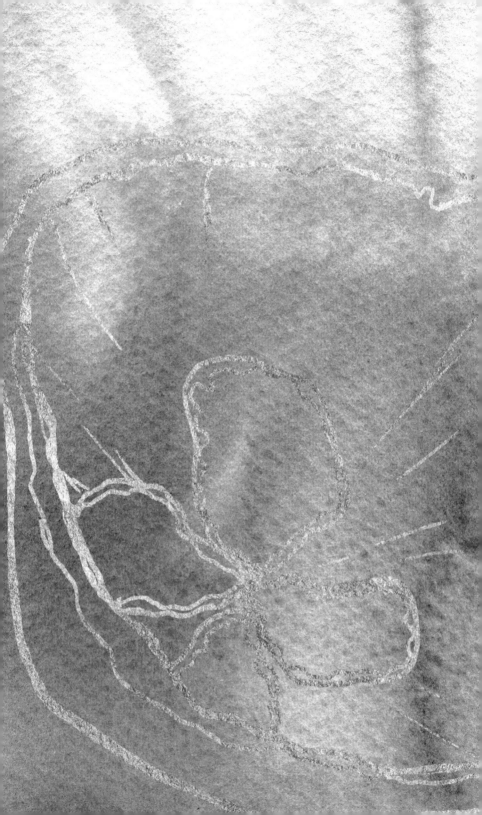

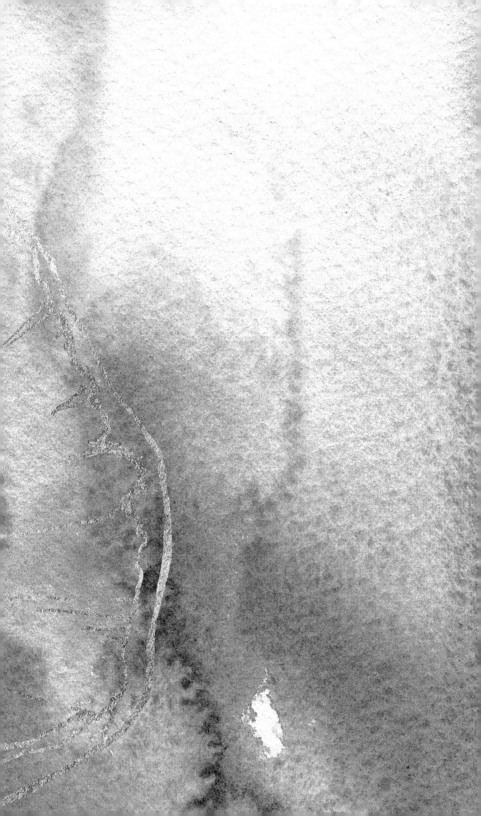

WE WELCOME TRAUMA LIKE A FRIEND

I have known trauma since
the day I entered this world; since
the umbilical cord wrapped itself around
my neck, turning brown skin
purple in the process.

I have befriended trauma
in the form of familial ties
and failed relationships. Sipped wine
with scuffed knees and bloody noses. Still,
I have risen, kept one foot in front of the other.

So, when you ask me how I
keep going on when hurt knocks
at my door, I only know
how to tell you that I welcome it
in like an old friend.

I learned along the way
to hold on to plans,
dig nails into the details,
leave no room for grey areas.

Living with OCD made it
easier (harder) to strive for this—
never knowing a moment's rest
until perfection was attained.

But the universe has a funny way
of knocking you to your feet, ripping
all your safe zones away
from your fingertips, teaching you
that, quite often, plans involving others
can quickly change.

I learned along the way
that grief holds as many lessons
in it as mundane life, and I am
learning each day how to get better
at saying goodbye.

—This is not a lesson I am good at

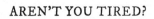

AREN'T YOU TIRED?

Aren't you tired, my dear?
How much longer can you hold it in?
It takes courage to carry this world
on one's shoulders. But, ever so often,
you are allowed to set it aside.

Isn't it exhausting, my dear?
The way you paint yourself to be so together,
yet fall apart as soon as you are behind closed doors.

Who taught you your value resided
in the ability to seem perfect?

Who required you to give
and give
until you depleted your reserves?
To never stop giving even when you do?

Tell me, do the ones who taught you this do it too?

Who taught you that you were not worthy
of love? Who taught you that you
weren't worthy of your own love?

Was it your mother and the way
she belittled you in every breath?

Was it your father, who was too upset
with you to say happy birthday?

Was it your schoolmates, who picked fun
at you like a scab, refusing to stop
even when blood broke the surface?

It must be so exhausting to plaster
a smile on your face without a drop
of life in your bones.

Tell me, isn't it time you spend
this much energy on yourself?

BE STILL, LISTEN

This kind of listening torments me:
the one that arises when I am in the middle
of traffic and wonder how quickly I can
kill myself. The kind of listening
that accompanies me throughout the day
during my mind's smooth coaxing to start trouble.

Go on, key the car

This kind of listening that stands at attention,
takes in its surroundings, does not retaliate

Break the windshield

The kind of listening that witnesses
the thoughts of anger, grief, sadness—observes.
Takes in the blows, does not react

What in the actual fuck?

This kind of listening, the one my therapist
tries to teach me, the noticing kind
that has evolved from the kind of listening
I taught myself when I was younger.

That kind of listening allowed me to be seen
and not heard. This kind of listening wants me
to stand tall in my "good" and "bad" thoughts.
To accept them as they are without a need
to identify with them.

This kind of listening torments me:
it takes too much energy to listen from a
place of recovery—it is much easier to
go through my days being depressed.

MAPLELEAF AVENUE

My eyes took in the living room:
a Christmas tree in the corner two months
before its time, adorned with bright
silver tinsel and the ornaments my mother
got from farin* last August.

I sit high on the pink tricycle, glide fingers
over its handles, down the length
of the white tassels.

The only memories I have of my childhood
are these and that time I removed putrid
vomit from my braided hair in the third grade.

My mother's love for Christmas is present
in me along with the inability to believe
someone could actually love me.

And it isn't her fault,
not entirely, because I not only have
my father's smile but, somehow, took on
his nature of keeping the peace to the point
I often sacrifice myself in the process.

The best and worst parts of my parents
exist within me like the way I try to be kind
to everyone, and the way my blood boils
when I am wronged.

The way I will give my last dollar to
someone in need, and the way I perceive
the world with my mental illnesses.

Despite their qualities in me, I hope I find
the courage to still be the little girl
on the pink tricycle: the one who fell, brushed
her knees off, got back on while crying,
always having the confidence to try once more.

---

*Caribbean saying: foreign. Often refers to America, but can mean
any country overseas (excluding any other Caribbean country)

BURN THE CURRY

My mother was the kind of woman who needed control. Turned summer breaks into home-school days led by a syllabus of her own making, gave a schedule for what we had to sit in our rooms and learn, set limits to the time we got to enjoy a television show, picked when and where we went out, kept us sheltered from the outside world.

Therapy taught me that generational trauma existed—how someone is formed based on the way they received love, or the lack thereof. Christianity and conservative Jamaica had a huge role in the passing down of these lessons. Unhealed trauma had a way of passing along in genetics and pushing your children off when they expressed affection. Fathers walking out and marrying another woman—raising her children instead—had a way of presenting itself in month-long arguments and enrolling your children in all-girls schools. Education was the most important thing. There was time for nothing more. Their God, their religion, taught me that I was unclean, made to have my skin burn in the pits of hell if I so much as loved someone with the same thing that was between my legs.

I often looked for love in people who rejected me. Rejected those who offered a sense of security and found homes in those that did not appreciate what I had to offer. My relationships became transactional in a sense, often resulting in me giving my entire being for half of a fraction of what I was receiving. The capitalistic society of my romantic partnerships led me to fall in love with a man who consumed me.

It started out as any other love story would: quickly, intensely, filled with butterflies, sweaty palms, days spent between sheets, and frogs settling into throats. What began as a summer fling quickly became something more. They say hindsight is often 20/20 and looking back at this (and most of my relationships), I should have known how it would end. His eyes always found something that was more. His reassurances fell on deaf ears, the beginning stages of OCD, a lifelong pattern of trauma and a crushing fear of abandonment. I should have anticipated the day he would have gotten her pregnant.

The few months after I last saw him, after I flew cross-country to a barren state of dying love and false promises, I decided to reparent myself. Took lessons from my therapist, media, self-help books, and close confidantes. I learned how to truly be alone, stumbled back into lessons after stumbling out of various placeholder's beds. The road to recovery is not a straight line and often looked like a series of mistakes followed by moments of clarity. The process involved me learning to cook and fend for myself for the first time in the midst of a global pandemic.

Alexander taught me a staple of my heritage. Stitched me back together with a simple recipe just months before he died. The task was simple: cut the meat into chunks, season with whatever your heart desired, let it sit overnight, grease the pan, burn the curry.

The term is a peculiar one, possibly unique to Jamaicans. Essentially, one burns the curry to release the flavour. Sets fire to something so critical in hopes of creating something new, something substantial. I have heard the term countless times, never truly understanding what it meant until that video call. The curry must disintegrate to become something more.

I learned how to make curry chicken that day. And though I have messed up countless times after that— forgotten the proportions, made it too watery—for the first time I cooked my own meal. Provided for myself in more ways than any other person had before.

Such a simple task started a revolution in me. Sometimes giving up control could look like falling, failing, crying on shower floors, wiping your tears and picking yourself back up, and making very watery curry chicken. I learned how to feel my feelings and embrace the tempest of this thing called life. It is when we succumb to the pain that it has a chance to transform into something new.

I still have a long way to go. Still have loads to learn about choosing myself time and time again, setting and maintaining boundaries, healing all that has come before me. However, I am no longer that girl who becomes devastated over someone who does not see her worth. I am no longer making myself small, dimming my light to let the light of others shine more brightly. I have risen out of the ashes like a phoenix; emerged as a woman who still loves wholeheartedly, in spite of what others have put her through, still coming home to myself in the midst of talking stages and failed situationships. I am no longer the girl who begged someone to stay. Begged them to choose me. Love me. Make me their home.

So, if you must do anything, do this:

Forgive yourself for being the person you had to be in that time. For accepting less than what you gave out. For acting in ways that traced back to the lands where your ancestors took their first breath.

Understand that it takes time to grow and heal and accept what you truly deserve.

Set fire to those old neural pathways and belief systems.

Have a funeral for the person you no longer wish to be.

And burn the fucking curry.

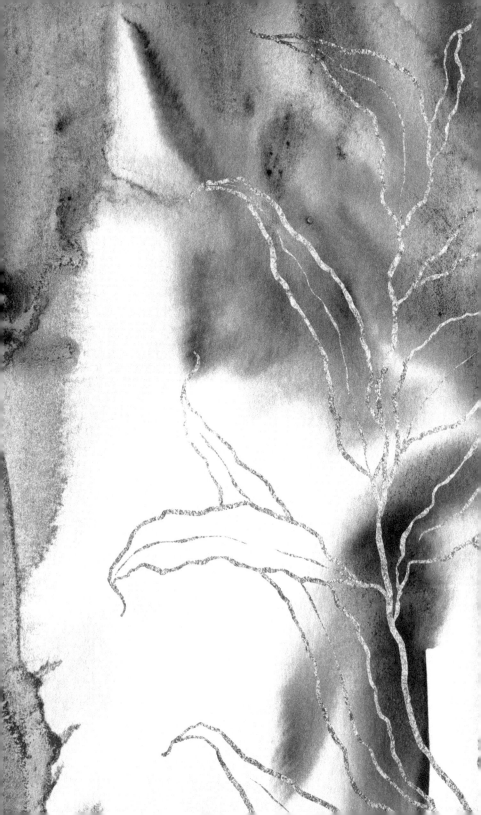

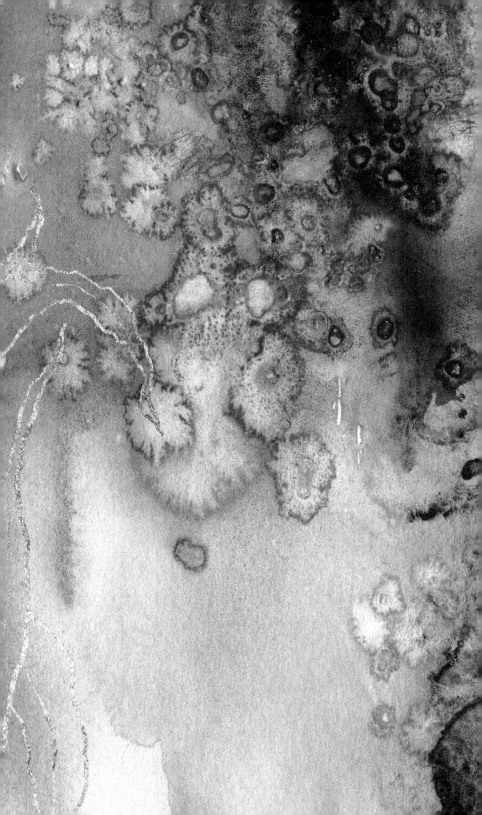

EULOGY

Here lies the bodies of the men I once loved,
put 6 feet below the ground before their time.
We gather here today to embrace their life, feast our eyes
on the good times (turn our gazes away from the bad). Remember the time
this one cupped my face between his hands and told me that
I made him the happiest person alive.
(Ignore that three days later he walked away because I did not give him sparks.)
And, here lies the body of the man I poured my soul into—
forget the fact that he impregnated another.
Here lies the man I adored, sat cross-legged on his bed
as he explained a card game to me.
Ignore the time he fucked me,
fucked his ex-girlfriend,
then made an honest woman out of another;
the time he told me he was celibate while fucking her.

We gather here only to muster up enough courage
to speak kind compassionate words; we are taught
never to speak ill of the dead.

Here lie the men I broke myself for;
may they never rest in peace.

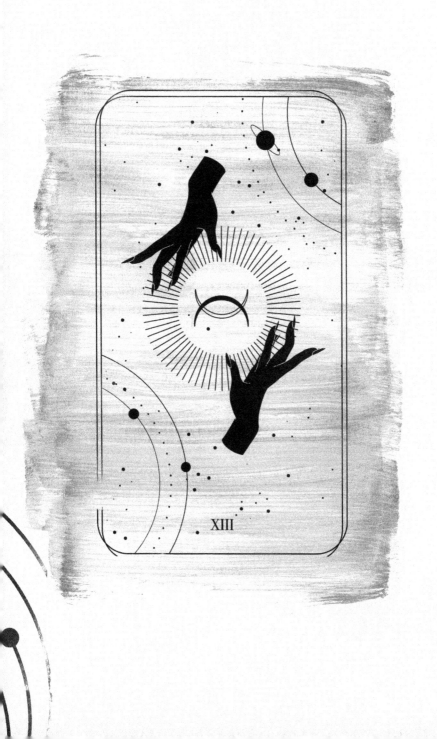

THE GALAXY OF US

I have learned to hold space
for the people I love—
step back and allow them to plant
their own seeds, harvest
their own fruit.

I have learned to extend a hand
when they need, assure them
that we can exist in this space
without my need to fix everything
overshadowing their need to just be.

There are times I falter, grasping
at control as a child does a butterfly.
But you can't tame a wild thing,
can't usher in the good times faster.
Because it is in our lows
that we appreciate our highs,
learn our lessons, grow.

I have learned to hold space
for the people I love. I am learning,
also, to hold space for myself—
become one of those people I love.

MOLEEN

She is clothed in strength and dignity and laughs without fear of the future"
- Proverbs 31:25

And if you were to bend over
at the waist, heave up your lungs in an
attempt to feel
     anything,
she would swoop in, wipe your tears,
straighten your armour.

Her hair curls without trepidation,
defines its growth like that
of the lotus; through harsh conditions,
it flourishes.

She tackles each day with the brightest
smile, shines light on all in her path, cares
for even the smallest on this Earth.

Through all of life's trials she comes out
stronger, and in the face of my own,
I am honoured to call her my teacher
and my friend.

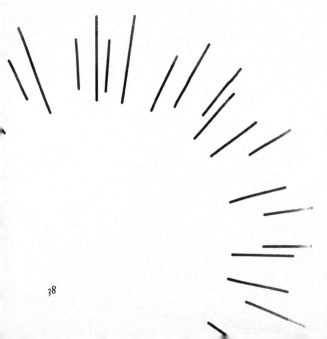

DOOMSDAY

It is currently 100 seconds to midnight
and I have spent more time learning
how to exist without you in this galaxy
than learning how to conserve energy.
Unfortunately, when it rains, my brain
can only concentrate on the contents
of my mug: coffee.

Do you still add cream, or is your coffee
now as dark as the midnight
hour? Because while I am learning
to make myself into myself, your energy
shifts to accommodate hers. The galaxy
of that pain magnifies as it rains.

But, I feel more in my power when it rains.
Since I was younger—nose deep in books learning
about fairytales, experiments, the galaxy,
hand around a cup of coffee—
I learned how to harness my energy
as my soul dived into the midnight.

That depth of the midnight
abyss brings about a plethora of learning,
growth, strength, and healing rains,
and if I am sure about anything, it's that my coffee
and storms become a force in this galaxy,
dependent on the influx of my energy.

So, while you give your energy
to the family you created, learn
how to be fine without me, share your coffee
with a woman who views me as the rains
of your past, the 100-second mark to midnight
before the implosion of her galaxy.

I stare up into this galaxy,
watch the moon strengthen as it rings midnight,
finger the pages of the book I am learning,
the one ran rampant with coffee
rings, read multiple times during summer rains.
I take back the promise of sharing my energy,

because now I understand that
the potential I once saw in you
was only what I would have done
given the same circumstances.

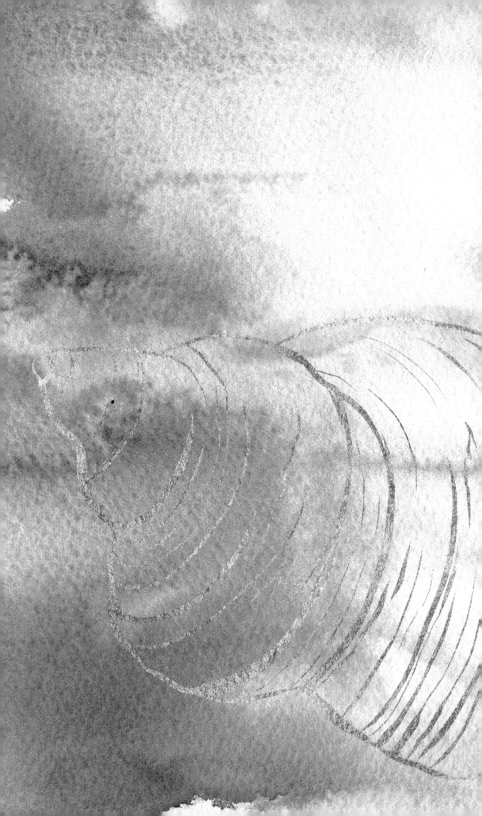

I have stains
on my shirts that
have lasted longer
than the men
I have encountered.

—take from that what you will

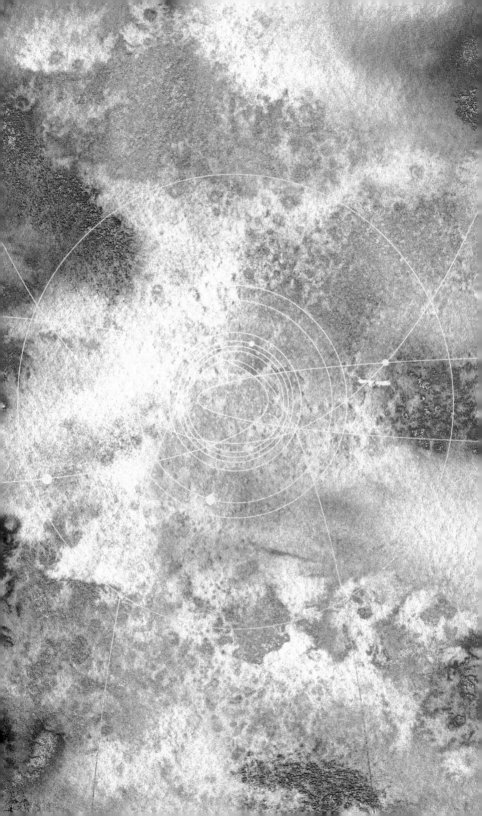

BONAVENTURE

I am waiting for the day when
my body feels less like a graveyard
where men cum then move on
to their final resting place.

I am waiting for the moment
I feel whole, able to sit on display
like a pile of ripe oranges
at the farmer's market, to be valued
for just being,
without subjecting my worth to what lies
between my legs.

The book of the undead changes in length,
the men of my past come in and out
(and I have to stop letting them).
Because isn't it sad how one's body count
goes from thirty to three
when you believe that
if you don't cum it doesn't count?

Understand this: I am trying to find people
who will play catch with my energy
rather than those who make it feel
like I am blowing bubbles with Death.

TO THE MAN HE CALLS HIS FRIEND

i)   The invalidation of my feelings is non-negotiable.

ii)   Spare me the broken record
of your subjective list of his accolades. Spare me
the details of the time he dropped everything
to help you build your gazebo.

iii)   Do not tell me that
life gets better because life
right now is pretty much bullshit.

iv)   Save the speech about
how good of a guy he is
despite the fact that he strung me along,
in spite of the fact he never intended
on loving me in the first place.

v)   I do not care how much you tell me
forgiveness is my way out of this;
he knew what he was doing.

vi)   You weren't there when he held my hand,
said he wished he had known
I felt the same way. You weren't there
when he made it seem like I was the only one.

vii)   Your outlook on this is subjective. You see
a good man who puts others' needs above his own.
I see a narcissist.

viii)   You don't get to tell me he is a good guy.

IT COMES IN WAVES

your face, your touch,
the way your skin smells
straight out of a shower—
eucalyptus and lavender.

I knit blankets to take
my mind off you,
loop thread through itself,
feel plush weigh itself down
in my palms.

I am slowly running out
of storage space.

WHAT AN AWFUL CURSE IT IS

TO BE THE ONE

WHO WILL

ALWAYS

LOVE MORE

It's funny how my life
has come down to three phrases
these days:

I miss you.

I want you.

I love you.

STORM

The causeway flooded today.
I had cancelled my appointment
to change my tires for the fourth time
this month, choosing to spend my days
under a blanket once more.

The tail of the storm
settled itself over our town, bringing
the marshes to life in the process.
I decided to brave the journey
across the bridges, two hands gripping
the wheel, thirty miles less than the speed
limit as wind beat against the body of my vehicle.

Tires coasted on water,
volume turned down, fog lights
illuminating nothing but pounding
heartbeats and racing thoughts.

I could die here
and you still wouldn't call.

DEAR DEREK, I THINK IT'S TIME WE BROKE UP

You taught me how a man
should love a woman, turned
post-it notes into lifelong promises,
elevator rides into moments
of professing love...

Love, to you, was easy, never
shying away from the dark, the twists—
ushering in moments of peace
and tranquility.

But, you see, I can't keep going on
like this, can't keep treating love
as if it were a fairytale ending. I can't
keep looking for you in other people.
Can't keep taking your love and adding
tax to it, presenting it to these real-world men.

For so long you were it.
Save for the time I casted my gaze
on the lanky agent who read books
as quickly as I read people.

Because no matter how many times
I turn the men that traversed into my life
into the sun, they quickly, and quite often,
showed me just how much they can disappoint me.

So, Derek, it was nice while it lasted.
But it's time that we go our separate
ways. Because real love is not filled
with butterflies and sparks, but a promise
to keep showing up. Or...
it comes in the form of broken promises
and shattered hearts.

WHILE LIVING WITH OCD

My therapist is trying
to teach me the ways of the grey—
not to think in black or white, but
to hold space for the middle ground
in hopes of mitigating the effects
of my OCD.

I found out you were dating
her today. Ignore the times
you reassured me that I was
the one despite not being
a skinny, blonde, white girl.

Ignore the moment you told me
that you did not know her.
Forget the fact that your office
chair brushed against hers when
you slid out from under your desk
for a cup of coffee. Forget I have
seen you smile from ear to ear
while talking to her.

Our friends say you are a good guy,
tell me it's just the way of the 22-year-old
to chase after sparks, run
towards chemistry instead of learning
the art of alchemy, shunning the work
of creating a lasting love—choosing,
instead, to settle into the rom-com
notion that love comes easy.

They tell me you are a good guy, but
I've seen the bad, broke down in my car
as I sped across the causeway
somehow hoping I could escape
from the problems that present
themselves on a daily basis, somehow
wishing that if my car went over,
you'd find it within yourself to know
that I was the one, that you made a grave
mistake.

My therapist is trying to teach me
the ways of the grey, because maybe,
sometimes,
even good people do bad things.

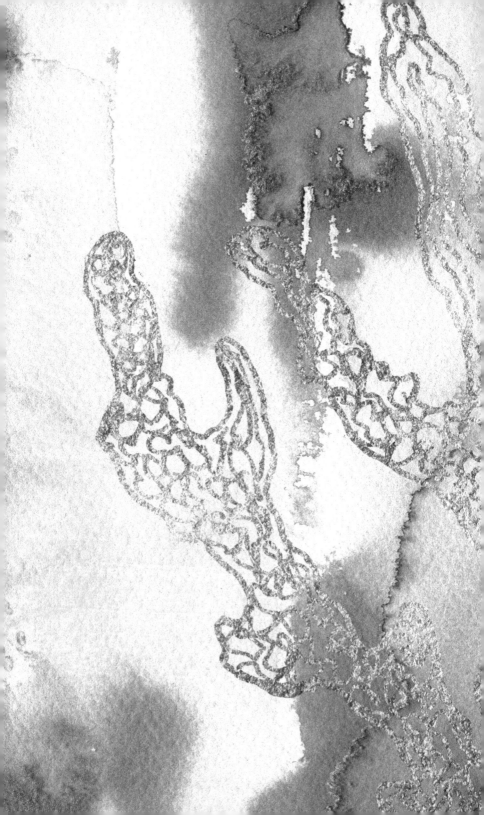

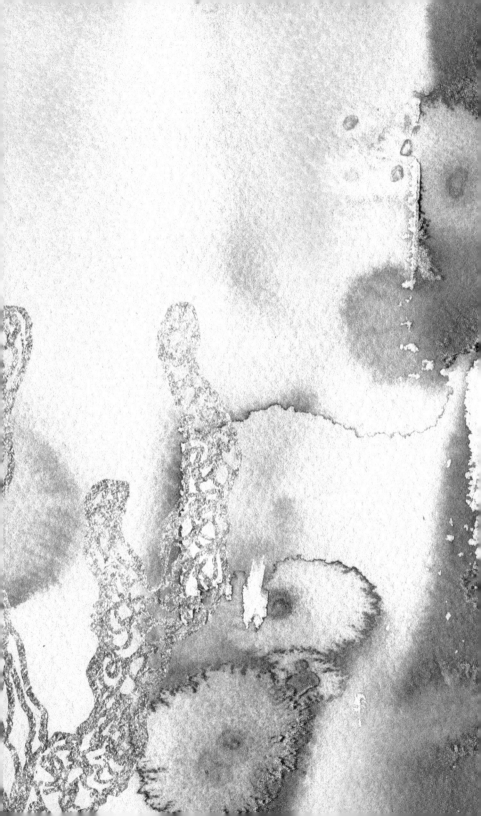

FREEDOM

I wanted everything out of life:
that was the problem.
I wanted both sides of the coin
at the same time, to have my cake
and eat it too. I wanted to be
wholeheartedly, unequivocally in love
and to be left the fuck alone.

I could never settle on one path:
I would be the world's first
chef scientist—skip past the part
where I could barely boil water;
ignore my failing grade in biochemistry.
My career choices became whatever
I could manage to focus on
at that second, fleeting away as quickly
as someone's last breath.

I, quite often, second-guess myself
into depression, have dinner
with imposter syndrome and afternoon
tea with anxiety. Choices are often
avoided—ironic for someone
with the pervasive need for control.

All I have known is that I wanted
freedom. Freedom to do, and say,
and be. Freedom to travel, love, learn,
grow and expand. And, quite often,
freedom looked like whatever
decision was in my best interest
at the moment.

Freedom, quite often, took the form
of lovers who meant me wrong;
a country, miles away
from my first breath,
where freedom became the home
I always searched for.

I WANTED A CHILD ONCE

My daughter jumps in my bed,
declares we are staying home and
taking a mental health day, orders
me to strip to my undies, scramble
some eggs, turn on Netflix for the day.

We build a fort in the living room,
gather all the blankets that don't need
washing, borrow the couch's pillows
and get close, breathe each other's air
as we laugh about something funny
she said (she's such a funny kid).

She is small but tough, grips
life by the balls, and when you see
her crying, bruised at the knuckles,
gutted by something or someone
life put on her path, she'll only tell you
"You should see the other guy!"

I see myself in her, see all the things
I wished for myself in her: her steady
nature, a force to be reckoned with,
how she meets life with arms wide open,
and does not shy away from failure.

And while I lay in this fort, back
pressed deep into grey carpet, stripped
down to my undies, scrambled eggs
cold on the plate beside me, Netflix
on in the background, I know
that if I ever had her, this is how
she would have been.

HINDSIGHT

I have tried time and time again
to plant you into the lovers
I have shared my bed with.

Convinced each one to purchase
the cologne I originally gave to you,
the one you made your own.

I have shared with them the same
secrets I once whispered in your ear,
spread my legs across their thighs
in the same way I once did with you.

Bought the same shirts, cooked
the same meals, wrote the same words
on the same pages I sealed
with a kiss, tied together with a bow
on birthdays and anniversaries.

Did my best to recreate a moment
(moments) I once had with you,
tried hard to muster up the same
feelings you once gave me.

But, they just aren't you,
and honestly, I am starting to think
I really don't want them to be.

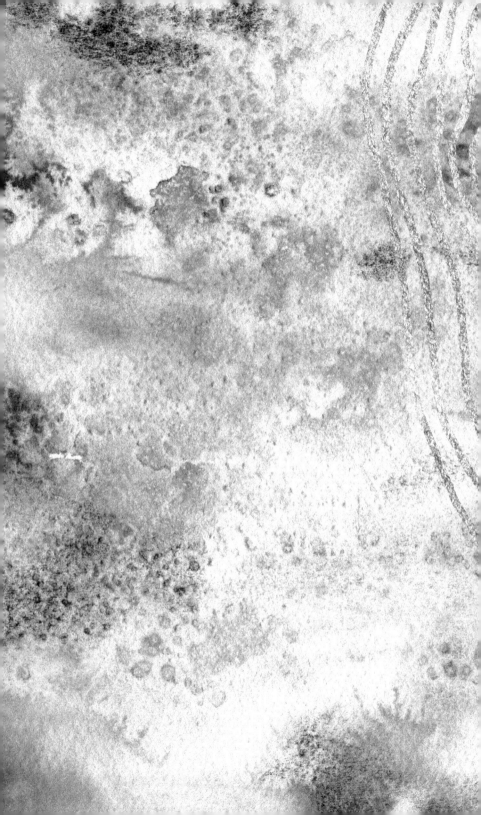

TWELVE THINGS I HAVE LEARNED ALONG THE WAY

1)   Never make a feast out of the crumbs someone else has given to you.

2)   You have spent enough time giving to others. It is time to give to yourself.

3)   Forgive yourself for the bad things you have done. Just because you have made mistakes, does not mean you are one.

4)   Stop worrying if other people like you. The most important thing to pay attention to is how you feel and what makes you happy.

5)   It is okay to grieve the living. Not everyone lives up to our expectations. That is okay. Take the time to feel what it is that you must feel.

6)   There will come a time when you must make your voice heard. Remember, you are allowed to take up space.

7)   Approach life from the stance that you do not know everything. It is okay to be a beginner.

8)   Stop taking on the weight of what is not yours. You are only responsible for your choices, your actions, your reactions. Someone else's problems, remarks, choices are not yours to deal with.

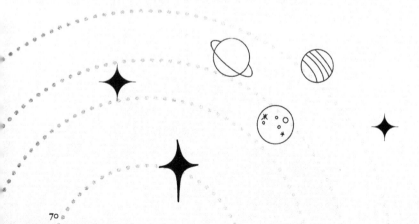

9)   If you do not want to forgive them (or can't),
      that is okay. It is possible to save it for another
      time. Just do not hurt yourself in the process.

10)   You can logically know that someone did their best
      in loving you and raising you and still not want
      anything to do with them.

11)   Do not become so accustomed to the bad that you
      seek it out when things go right.

12)   Recovery is not a straight shot from point A
      to point B. You are allowed to make twists and
      turns, go backwards and forwards as
      much as possible. It gets easier with time.

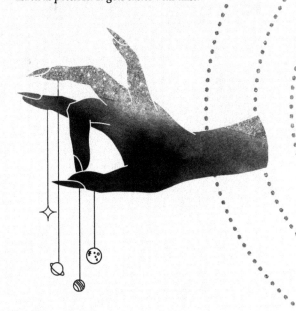

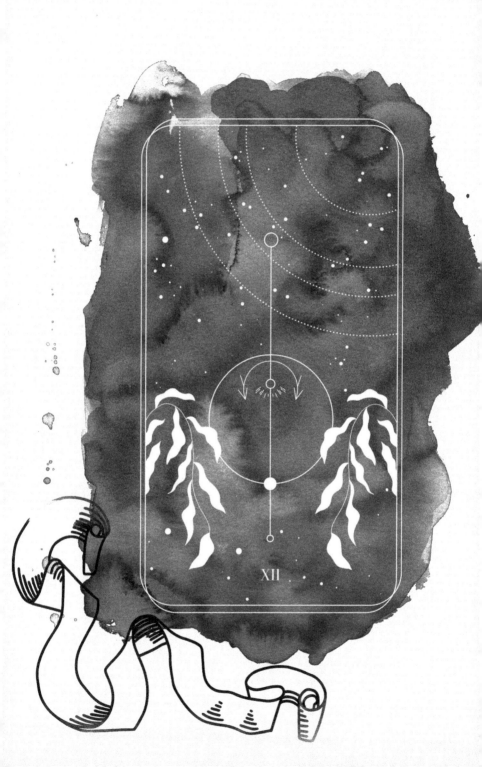

IN DEPRESSION'S ARMS

Seven coffee mugs litter
the living room table,
still half-filled with creamed
coffee and specks of mold.

Yesterday, I finally made my way
through the piles of laundry,
tossed them all into the machine
overloaded with soap, decided
against separating like I always do.

Today's tasks are simple: wash the mugs,
wipe down the table, put away the
clothes. I sit on the grey suede couch,
stare at four black mugs—three multi-coloured,
two piles of clean laundry and the
disinfecting wipes.

Seven years ago, I graduated with honours,
moved thousands of miles away from home:
alone, afraid, but independent.
Today, I sit here on this grey couch,
surrounded by tasks a child could handle,
with no energy to do any of it,
with nothing left within me.

This is to say, my life has come down
to these few things lately, and I don't
particularly know how to keep on
living.

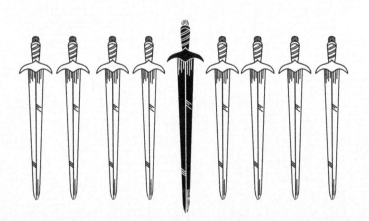

RECIPE FOR ME

Various versions of myself
exist within the minds of many
I have loved before. And there lies
the problem, for I have exchanged
my love like currency, often giving
out twice-fold for even the smallest
transaction. In the minds of some,
I am an enigma; in the minds of others,
a bitch, and, still, in the minds of
a few, the one who got away.
I have never been one familiar
with savings, and, quite often, one
familiar with depletion. It's funny
to see one whittle themselves
down to nothingness to
keep other people happy. It's
funny that I know nothing about
having a fund for emergencies.
Does numbness count
as an emergency? Or just another
step in this life? I am slowly trying
to pick apart who it is I truly am from
who other people think I am, from
what I have portrayed myself to be
in hopes of hiding the scared girl.
And I keep coming up with
an empty shell. But it's a little
reassuring that the best things
are often made from scratch.

INSECURITIES

Was I too soft for you?
Slipped through your fingers like putty,
only to be tossed aside, all dried out
and dirty.

I have religiously identified too deeply
with being abandoned, often announcing
my intentions before the passengers
in my vehicle have any doubts.

You see, I have become too
accustomed to being the victim, going
to therapy, being the one who is always left.

I am terrified that this is all I will be.

I am terrified that I am the one who chose
to be this way.

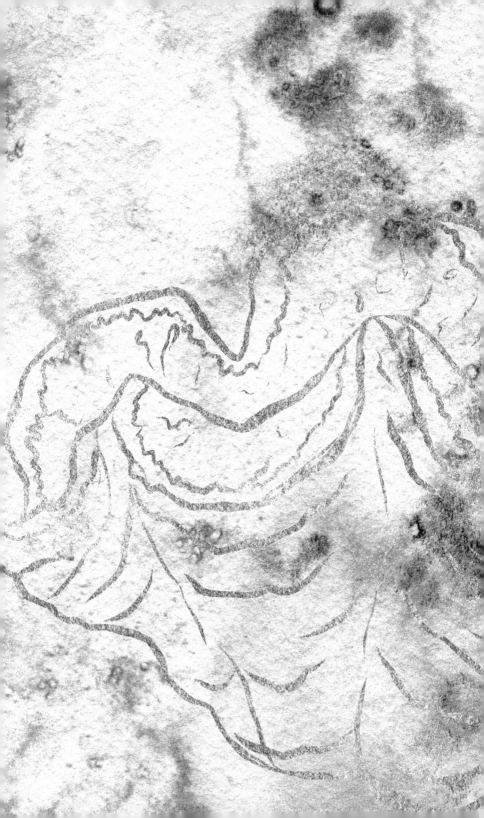

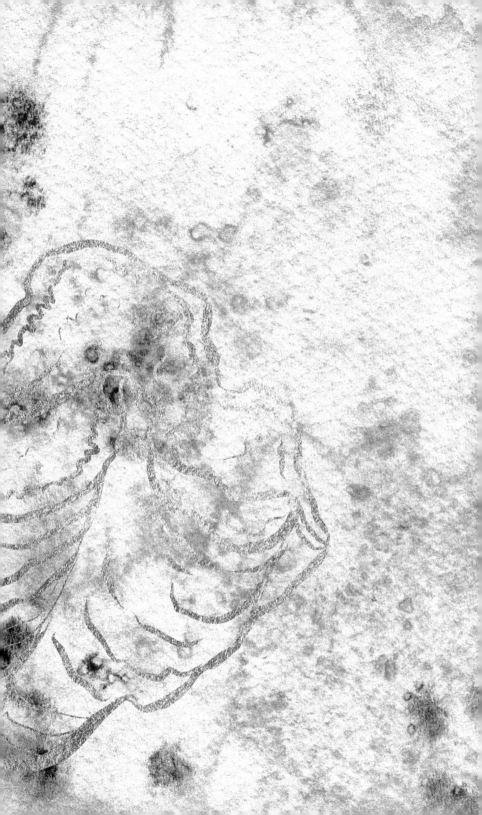

I AM LEARNING NOT TO DEFINE MYSELF
BY WHAT HAPPENED TO ME

The night was still, more so than usual.
The red boxer that often stood guard,
waist height, always doing his business
on the small patch of lawn, appeared
to be in his apartment, probably under
the covers, getting ready for bed.

Curtains were drawn, light glowed through
as best as it could. The streetlamp flickered,
as it often did. The inhabitants quieter
than usual; the parked black car took
in every detail.

I moved as quickly as I could, barefoot
against the pavement, up onto the sidewalk,
into the townhouse with the red door,
turned the lock, checked it thrice.

My knee stung as I climbed each step,
blood trickled from the flesh-coloured wound.
Did the carpet always feel this soft?
Did the fifth step always creak?

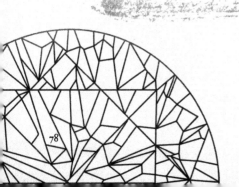

I woke at 6am the next morning,
unsure of what occurred last night after
it happened. The bandage now had a mixture
of pus and blood—was that even possible?

I stepped into the shower, undid my pineapple,
let the water run over my head, stood there
for thirty minutes until I felt like the soap
had done what it was supposed to, then restarted
the process, rewashed the spots that no longer felt
like my own, could no longer be my own.

People have a way of claiming what isn't theirs—
quite often forcefully, quite often disguised
behind the notion that you started by giving consent.

And maybe this is why, a year later,
I still have trouble calling it rape.

LEARNING TO LET GO

We do not know how to let go
of beautiful things—things we define
that way.

On my dresser, I have several rocks—
ones I defined as pretty along the way.
The blue one I bought at the spiritual
shop on the island, the one in between
the sushi place and Wine Alley.
The pink one I got from Etsy, the white
one from the bridge.

Mugs from museums, coffee shops, Target,
thrift shops and galleries—even the one
with the chip and crack is still there.

I kept the blue dress two sizes too small
because it was too beautiful not to have,
and the chain with St Francis, though we
don't speak much anymore.

We seldom know how to let go of beautiful
things—well, I seldom do. I hope I learn
how to only hold on to what is important.

I am learning how to accept
apologies that will never come my way,
learning to grieve those still living,
and learning that doing so
does not make me any less entitled
to the salvation that may come as a result
of the trauma I was burdened with in the process.

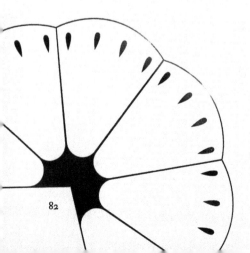

HANDS

I don't believe I was meant to be born. Or, rather, maybe I was meant to be born chasing something else.

I took my first breath with my father on the ground, eyes closed, passed out from witnessing the blues and purples of my face, moon-shaped alien head, umbilical cord wrapped tight like an old wedding ring around my neck.

I chased my first thing that day—breath. Let out a wail so loud that everyone in the ward knew I was alive.

I chased my mother's legs when I learned to walk, held on to navy blue pant legs when she came home from work, chased my sister around in hopes of being her friend.

Ran after grades and degrees as if they were going extinct.

Chased boys and girls in hopes that they would love me.

Someone once told me that the open palm knows more strength than the closed fist. Calluses and hardened skin somehow meant more than bruised knuckles and broken fingers. When you break your thumb, you know what not to do next time. When you open your palm, and it gets rejected, it takes everything within you to keep on opening it.

Because even though I don't think I was meant to be born, I think I was meant to be chasing something—I hope I continue opening my palms to this world, chasing even the smallest ray of light.

I SPENT YEARS LEARNING HOW

TO RECOGNIZE

THE SOUND OF MY VOICE,

I'LL BE DAMNED IF ANYONE EVER

SILENCES ME AGAIN.

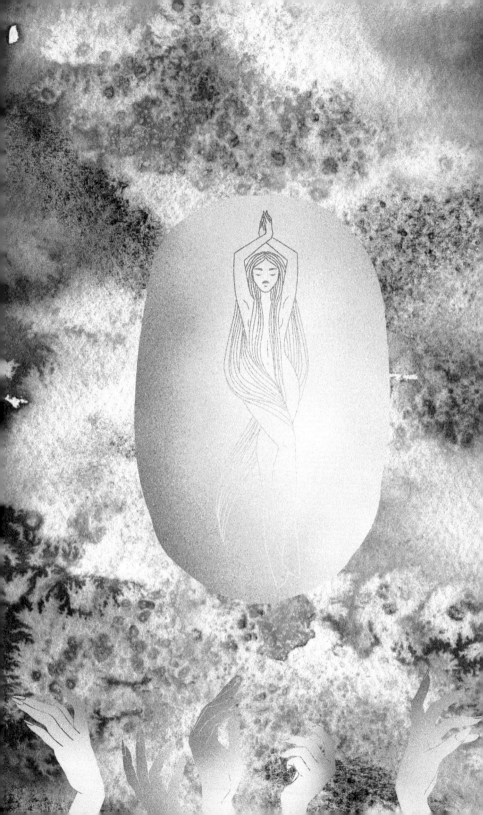

RIO COBRE

There is this tale in Jamaica, one of a golden table—the kind of tale mothers and teachers tell children in hopes of teaching them a deeper meaning.

The golden table is a sight to see, often emerging from the Rio Cobre at noon on the hottest day of the year. The river holds many secrets and, as the tale has it, the bodies of those who have tried to retrieve the table from the river.

We are a people who are friendly with want. We want for things we cannot have, things we can, and things we are better without.

I have come across my own golden tables in this lifetime. The man with the charm, the girl with her collection of beer bottles, the boy in the body of a man. Each one beautiful, each one surfacing in the river of my life, each one pulling me below the surface as quickly as they appeared.

I, too, have been like these people. Been the golden table in the river of someone else's life. Broken hearts and left bitter tastes in mouths along the way—caused people to drown as I took them down.

My birth chart says I will have a hard time in this life with individuality, have a hard time allowing people to be as they are. Allowing myself the freedom to be as I am.

Maybe this is why I have taken people down into the depths with me. Drowning them and playing the victim. Because I know not what it means to be alone. Or, rather, I am too afraid to find out.

And it isn't the kind where one can't be by themselves, more of the kind where you feel as though you will never *truly* experience a sense of home—belonging.

I am learning to be the kind of woman who shimmers like the golden table, and the kind of woman who stands back, is present, admires other golden tables without a need to conquer. I am learning how not to drown or be drowned. How I can become one with myself and allow others the courtesy of being themselves.

WHAT WE LEARN AS WE GO

I like to think I am the kind
of girl people write poetry about.
But for years I taught myself
I was the kind of girl people
are only entertained by, then
tossed on the sidewalk
when they have had enough fun.

I like to think I am graceful, like
those dancers on the tips of their toes.
But I have stumbled out of bed
four times this week, with drool
running down the side of my mouth
and, quite often, trip over air.

I want to say I am strong, built
with high-strength concrete, the kind
that withstands category five hurricanes.
But I have become best friends
with the inside of my closet—too often
retreating there to hide from the world.

We learned in English class the definition
of a paradox—how two things can be
contradicting yet true. I like to think
I am a walking paradox. I have the ability
to be the one people write about
even though they only spend
five minutes with me.

NEAR DEATH EXPERIENCES

The truck with the Florida license
plate sat still at the red light. Packed
with logs and trunks ten sizes bigger
than me. They swayed in the back
as we took the right turn together.

Both of my hands are on the wheel;
nerves have made themselves known.
We take each turn together—
right, left, left, right, circle around,
emerge on the causeway.

I imagine one breaking loose
from the straps that hold them down,
imagine the log fitting like a puzzle
piece into my windshield,
into me.

We go over the first bridge together—
the water below is browner than usual—
marsh water collaborating with ocean.
I wonder if I may blend in with this
shade of brown if my car goes over
and I sink below the surface.

We approach the second bridge,
boats docked at the marina; the white
boat has tied up its sails today. If I turn my wheel
right, I wonder if I will end up
in the boat or in the brackish water below.

The truck now turns left. I continue straight
onwards to meet up with friends at the art show,
take on the shops at the pier, create memories.

For someone who wants to experience life
in all its glory, I sure do think of death a lot.

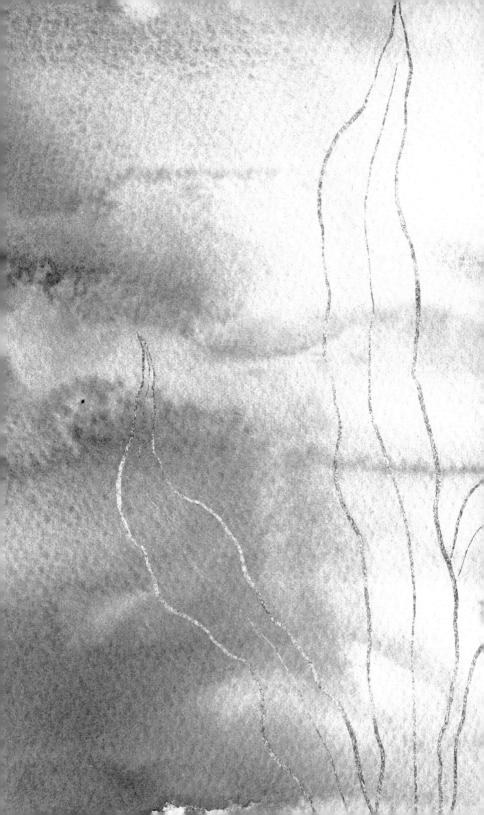

I have to keep reminding myself
that I cannot love a person into
loving me—can't manifest their text,
can't request the Universe to show
me signs of their true feelings
and then ignore the ones I don't like.

It has dawned on me that no answer
is, in itself, an answer—often the loudest
one. I can't love someone into
choosing me.

VI

There are a few things that have
broken my heart over the years:

      i.   The day Alex died
      ii.   The day I realized the light in my eyes had died
      iii.   Every time I have ever been cheated on
      iv.   "I give my heart away very fast,
                   but no matter how hard I tried,
                   I could never give it to you"

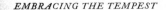

SAVANNAH, GA

I have taken the time to explore.
Not as much as I would like, but enough
to keep the illusion of freedom going.

He came into my life at a time
I had decided I wanted to do more,
see more, be more, live more,
love more.

As a child I constantly called myself
a nomad, often referring to home
as wherever I rested my head. I often
followed the path led by the compass
of my heart.

He took my hand, led me across
city lines to where our travels began.
A city inundated with history, stitched
together by cobblestone roads
and plastic cups of alcohol.

We became us there.
Understand that this is what I dreamed of,
a life of sightseeing and adventures, often
packed into geocaches and hiking boots.

I am more of myself now in his presence,
more of the woman I longed to become,
less of a nomad who changes her residences
like she changes her underwear, more of
a woman who knows when to call home.

I have found and built a home
with the man I love, in the man I love.
And though I am not friends with certainty,
I do hope we figure things out as they come.

THE STOLEN WALLET

The security guard looks up from his desk,
takes me in for the third time today. Face
withered away with wrinkles, each line
a year he spent serving in the border patrol.

I urge him to scan through the videos,
watch frame by frame of the back dock
from last Tuesday. I plead with him as he
hesitates, begging for him to overlook
the hours he will spend on this task and
focus on helping me.

*Maybe we could see if they threw my wallet
in the bushes or the dumpster.*

Desperation claws at my throat as the muscles
tighten. I am finding it hard to speak
without my voice breaking. Nails dig
deeper into my palms and I am surprised
no blood forms at the surface.

The contents of the missing wallet are as follows:

    1)   My social
    2)   My TRN*
    3)   My IDs
    4)   My insurance cards

My whole life is in there. Please.

It's funny how my identity has come down
to this—several cards placed purposefully
into their respective slots of the black wallet.

How my identity in this foreign land
is more along the lines of tangible things,
numbers, and coloured identification cards.

I have always had trouble answering the question
"Who am I?" and as I make the police report,
list the contents of my wallet to the officer,
I begin to wonder who I really am,
become grateful that the list of missing
items isn't as follows:

1)   A heart that keeps on loving even when it is wronged
2)   A mind that hungers for knowledge from any location
3)   A soul that believes in being kind and
       continuing to shine even in the darkest hour

*TRN: Tax Registration Number; sort of an equivalent to
the United States Social Security Number

Dear Love,

       I have asked you four times this week if I am annoying you. I, somehow, have served myself a five-course meal of anxiety over the years and I often wonder if I am not enough.

I am well aware you are not them, not the men and women of my past, but a whole new being entirely. But my eyes can no longer see with 20/20 vision when it comes to matters of the heart, and I am often inundated with thoughts and feelings that I will soon be left.

My therapist calls it relationship anxiety...
(noun): feelings and thoughts of worry or insecurities that present themselves in a relationship, even when things seem to be going well.

And things have been going well—the efficient communication, the actions that match the words, the love between us. But I can't help but feel as though one day you will wake up and feel nothing more for me, as though you will think you made a huge mistake.

I am not entirely sure why I think this way, why I have these deep feelings of abandonment. Why I feel as though I am good enough only for sex and not for a healthy relationship. I gather it has something to do with nature and nurture. Been to enough therapy sessions to understand that my experiences have created this core belief.

Logically, I know this.
Emotionally, I often forget it.

I am tired and a creature of habit. And this is not an excuse, not a way to forgive my issues, but a way to shed light on them. Because feelings of safety are terrifying for me. I do not know the first thing about having a healthy relationship.

So, I sit, observe, process, retreat into myself quite often because I am terrified the other shoe may drop. I am riddled with all manner of anxiety at the months we have spent together, happy. Even when we have argued, I have wondered if it would be our last fight. Because I love you and I am terrified that I cannot hold on to the people I love. Because certainty and I don't particularly see eye to eye, and you are someone worth having in my life.

So, when I ask for the fifth time if I annoy you, I am sorry. Trust me, I am working on it. Trust me, I am aware of my issues and doing my best to stop asking these questions—to become okay with the uncertainty that this life is often known for. Know that the anxiety has arisen because I fear losing you. I am learning how to love without tying someone down, without suffocation, learning to love someone else while dealing with the issues I have.

Please, be patient with me.

Love,

D. A.

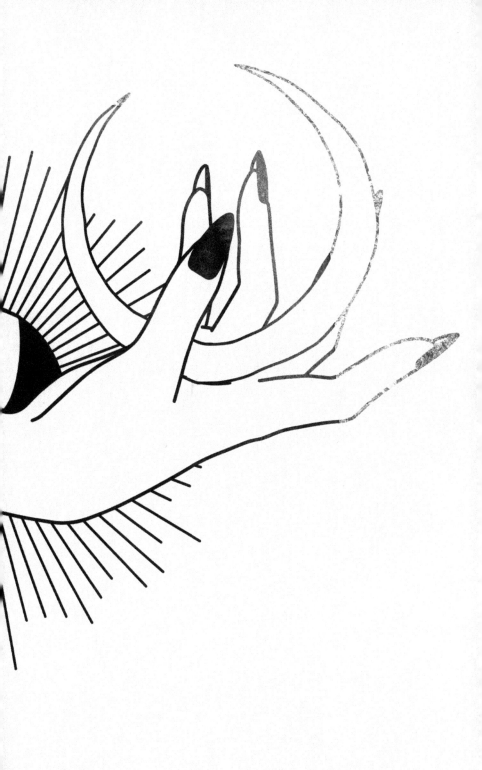

Thank you for taking the time to read my work!

I appreciate you and hope that you enjoyed it
and, at least, felt seen.

I ask that you leave a honest review if you
feel compelled to do so.

If you would like to follow me on my writing journey
and my day-to-day shenanigans, you can follow me on
Twitter, Instagram, and TikTok

@daandrews_

With love and light,

D. A. Andrews

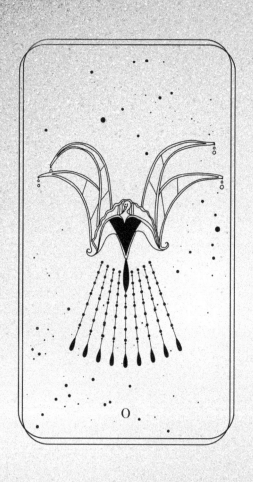

O

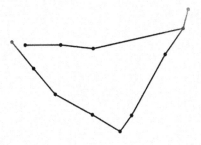

ABOUT THE AUTHOR

D. A. Andrews was born and raised in Kingston, Jamaica. Throughout the years, she has developed wide interests in various aspects of life, such as coffee, event planning, books, and psychology. She is a graduate of the University of the West Indies, Mona Campus with a BSc. in Marine Biology and Psychology (Honours) and is currently pursuing her MBA. She considers herself a nomad at heart and has changed cities and apartments quite as often as she changes her clothes. She is currently resting her head in Brunswick, Georgia, with her black cat, Luna and the newest addition, a puppy named Geaux.

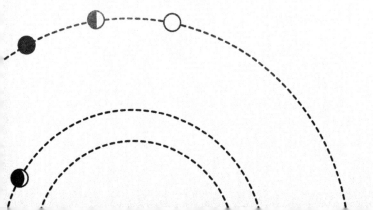

CPSIA information can be obtained
at www.ICGtesting.com
Printed in the USA
BVHW021801150722
642152BV00025B/1021